STONE SIGHTINGS

Canada Council   Conseil des Arts
for the Arts   du Canada

The publisher gratefully acknowledges the support of the Canada Council for the Arts for its publishing program.

The publisher is also grateful for the kind support received from an Anonymous Fund at The Calgary Foundation.

Library and Archives Canada Cataloguing in Publication

Sonik, Madeline, 1960-
        Stone sightings : poems / by Madeline Sonik.

(Inanna poetry and fiction series)
ISBN 978-0-9782233-9-7

        I. Title. II. Series.

PS8587.O558S74 2008   C811'.6   C2008-901881-8

Cover design by Val Fullard
Interior design by Luciana Ricciutelli
Printed and bound in Canada

Inanna Publications and Education Inc.
operating as *Canadian Woman Studies/les cahiers de la femme*
210 Founders College, York University
4700 Keele Street
Toronto, Ontario M3J 1P3 Canada
Telephone: (416) 736-5356 Fax (416) 736-5765
Email: inanna@yorku.ca Website: www.yorku.ca/inanna

Dear Heal,

2t wor a great fr every!
hope we do this again

STONE SIGHTINGS

poems by Madeline Sonik

December 20 2011

inanna poetry & fiction series

INANNA Publications and Education Inc.
Toronto, Canada

For my friend and daughter,
Madeline

Contents

Stone Age

Can I put this on your book, he grunts,
four hotdogs in a chrome pan
four buns, two knives
half a pound of butter
The Cradle of Civilization;

the wine mineralizes before a chemical log
growing steady with blue and orange spikes

upstairs our daughter blows out birthday candles
the clan deafens with heavy metal
thumps into Cambrian carpet
drummed with naked feet.

I fall asleep and dream of stampeding bison,
wild elk, the charcoal etch of antlers on loud white
stucco
my daughter's soft face
turning like a page
turning to stone.

Satellite

for Madeline

Last night I dreamed you lay in my lap
your head against the soft fabric of my thigh

you asked me questions:
why does the moon shine?

Your voice small, how I loved you there
and thought perhaps we could go back to this

when I could answer all your questions
and always you would answer me
and always I would answer you
when you could answer all my questions

and thought perhaps we could go back to this
my voice small, how you loved me there

why does the moon shine?
I asked you questions:

my head against the soft fabric of your thigh
last night you dreamed I lay in your lap.

Ties

Off the coast of Alaska
where water is striped
                    charcoal blue
and the sky a series of sinter,
a family of commorant wolves
noctivagate the land for food.

There are two mothers and fathers
two pups who for two years
have been cherished and guarded
Alaskan gold
curled in the warmth
of their family's pelts
kissed and cleaned
rough-and-tumbled
taught in the tribal knot
of their kin to
avoid the clutch
of king crab

to eat slippery blackfish
whole
to ring brown bear
in ropes of commotion.

For two years
they are tied

to the teat of their pack
carried by the scruff
of this nexus
until the auroral flash of adolescence

carried by scents
they swim the boreal ocean
silver paws
scraping
              forward
in a single
dogged
blaze.

Liberation

You didn't wave
through the blinds
as we pulled away

but we waved to the house front
to the withered weeds
the gnarled neglected leaves
that trembled down
brown like thrushes;

it was good, we said,
you didn't need to say good-bye,
didn't need us;

we talked about it all the way
to the ferry,
waived acknowledgement
for independent love—

it was good to leave you
knowing you didn't care.

Doing Daughter Differently

If I had the chance to do it differently
I would have my daughter at home
not in the hospital
name her Kate
not Madeline
and never have an ultrasound
prior to her birth.

I would refuse to buy her
pink toys
make sure she got the chance
to cry a little in her crib
later when she wanted an allowance
I would insist she work for it
change sheets
fold clothes
put her dolls away.

I wouldn't let her taste sugar
until she was twenty-one
or allow her to decide
anything for herself
until she moved out
and even then, I'd find a way
to make her come back to me
like Persephone
in the Spring.

Cleaning

Throw out
the paper pictures

that grinning
snake-mouthed sun
saying
I Love You—

at four you knew
the face of nature
wore it as you arabesqued
across the room;

here are your slippers
useless now as two small cows
who have calved
and grown hard as shells
with no milk left
to soften them

rubble of memories
scrape cobwebs and dust
from all these broken frames

so much bramble
grows   up
          between

mothers and daughters
to anchor us to the earth
and each other
we hold on
to everything

as if it were love
and gravity
that can't be trusted
to do their chores.

Clean

Bitterness can only enter
a woman's soul
if her house is clean,

the hours
scrubbing defoliated flesh
from the bathtub

are enough to make her want
to hold her daughter's heart

and the fornicating
hair and dust
balling
in the corners

will clamp her thighs
so tightly
against her husband
that in the epidermis
of dust she leaves behind
no living passion
will survive

but on her grave
they will write:

HERE LIES
A WOMAN WHO LIVED
IN A VERY CLEAN
HOUSE

God bless the women who are merciless

like my mother
throwing away
the toys I loved best;

how I cherish that wound
in explaining
my fears,

that pink blanket
shed of its ribbon
disappearing the night before

kindergarten
so I would have
nothing soft to hide beneath
or hold
or press
against my cheek,
and that same year
the glass bottle
I still hear breaking

like the sound of death
in soapy water
its dark brown nipple glistening

my mother's hand explaining

over unstoppable tears
how illegal it was

to sell bottles
to families without babies;
would I still

be drinking from that bottle
if she had been more compassionate,
agreed to my illicit plan

found a family
with a baby
who would lie
and break the law
for the desperation
of one weeping
suck.

Cause and Effect

she is afraid to leave her house
open her solid oak door
the street's glistening, desolate
width she must cross to get to the shopping mall
oceans of emptiness, untenable laws
she must cross, her own smallness
her own inability to change the
privilege in which she's stuck
the cross she pastes over the threshold

she can not buy the things she wants

if napalm and poison gas
did not fall, if small grass huts
did not implode and children
did not become swollen-bellied skeletons
someplace in the world
with wooden markers on their graves
nothing would bar her passage

but this spell
is something her too solid flesh
will not open, something
she is afraid to leave her house
to uncover

She scrubs her hands

checks to see the door is locked, the stove is off
one hundred times she checks
and finds herself checking again, counting
each time she returns and touches the light switch
behind the lamp, each time she thinks
of fire, scrubs her hands, happens over a crouching
man
who stepped into the living room
uninvited
collected the sky blue Wedgwood
her mother left behind in autumn
1989, the baby was two and still turning
that colour with seizures,
"nobody knows the trouble
I've seen," she sings, checks the stove
checks the door, washes her hands
counts the vowels and syllables
the notes that endlessly play

the door
the stove
her hands
the light switch

Legend

I washed the floor
in the blood of my grandfather's
amputated leg
wondering why I could not
move forward

the bread he made
lay in the blood
it would not reach my lips
but turned green like dying flesh
in my fist

My Joy is Darkness

The night I ran
through the neighbourhood
only white pickets of fences
glowing, the moon
shimmering on my flesh
a wrap of foil
over my wrist
the grass, seeming
freshly cut, though in fact
there had been frost
that morning, running
ringing door bells, in the
blackness, howling
at the fullness
of the night, the trick-or-treat
bag, swinging
for that moment
flickering like a tea light
in a jack-o-lantern
dark, my cloak, my robes,
scratching road like obsidian flint
over and over the stripe
of curb, over the seams of steps
sweet candy could never be
as bright a joy
as the darkness of that night.

The Little Match Girl

The trilling flame
that skipped from her match out of the fairytale book
was my gift

it came from my aunt and uncle
who had a penchant
for buying dangerous toys

my brothers got bows
and real arrows
the tips so sharp
they summoned rivers of blood
while I swam in a blue vinyl armchair
next to the shimmering Christmas tree

my terrified five-year-old eyes frozen
to read:
dying is vastly preferable
to being unloved.

One Tall Man

You carried me on your shoulders
told me to take the moon
my small arms stretching
over mountains to retrieve
that perfect circle glowing
a phosphorescent ball
I do not remember my age then
only that the Christmas tree
stood like a finned green rocket
   —dinosaur I'd called it that
awed by how tall it stood;
each year thereafter
the Christmas trees grew smaller
and the moon
rolled further away.

Fade

The gentle cows kicked against
their circles of shadow
shouting for me to turn on lights
moments before I played in gold
forgetting
I had run from the barn
fearful of darkness too.

My father never heard cows shouting—
he was deaf to certain sounds
a stranger in the world
of beasts he'd set
his life upon.

Each night and day the same
to him, each season
merging cows and children
dragging like plows over
fields.

His hands
never felt fear or
knew the white-faced cows'
uneasy wonder
at blackness.

His hands
never touched
sadness and never
called for light to enter
the world.

Looks

My father suited
in black pinstripes
extends to the end
of a six-foot cracker—in stocking feet
hollow cheeks thickened with cotton
balls and flesh tone
paint, Ukrainian women
I have never seen, holding
five star whiskey, wearing
garlic, they kiss and pinch
his bashful face
stroke his lineless forehead, wavy hair
raise the five star in thick
glass bells and stare.

He appears as he did
twenty years ago in a colourized
photo on grandma's T.V.
(he bought everything in twos
one for us
one for her)
beside the rabbit ear antennas
the painted wooden doll
who opens and spills
a crowd of miniature hers.

It is Christmas
a holly berry wreath
encircles my throat and spreads
along the optic nerve
destroying my vision
while Ukrainian women
ply me with amber vials,

"Drink," they are
wearing black babushkas
that look like tar paper
"Na zdorovye."

"Your father will always
be a handsome man."

Good Looking

You always say
you're not

bypassing those mirrors
in that stricken girl's face

whose heart sweats
over your shadow.

What do you see of yourself
in the polished surface of a table

or the cool flat reflector of water?
She is falling all over herself

not to fall over you

not to fall
and drown in your eyes

and hands
she wants to kiss

watching
for their touches

and stops herself
as you lean away
from brushing her lips
over the hairs on your arm

and wonders where you're looking
when you say you're not

beautiful, she would look there too
if only she could see another way.

eye (i)

It began wIth my body
droppIng out from under me
In some famIly crIsIs i can't recall whIch one
just as If a trap door
opened and i fell through

afterwards my chIldren and husband saId
you have become dIfferent, eerIly detached
they pIcked me daIsIes from the garden
brought mIlk chocolates to my bed

when they left
i examIned my body
notIced the flesh growIng thIn
the arms and legs smoothIng
to bone, mergIng
to dust

i looked Into the mIrror
and blInked
nose lIps haIr forehead
meltIng away
cheeks carved Into throat
throat Into chest
chest Into thIghs
wIth a mouth, i could scream at least

but i had become an eye
only an eye, just one great bIg fuckIn' eye

gazIng out, blInkIng
starvIng for vIsIon

eye (ii)

as an eye, eye get hungry
so hungry, that if eye had a mouth
eye would eat a telephone
savour the sweet white plastic or its casing
relish the twirling noodle cord delicacy
the coppery tang of tangled wire offal
oh with a little salt and pepper
fried in butter, that succulent mouth and ear pieces
brown
melt the digits
like heavenly bursts of inspiration
push buttoning the tongue to satiation
once digested
the best part
nothing would ever need to be communicated again.

The First Swan

I found her beneath the paving stone
after an evening
when words were not enough
to shape from clay
one feather;

she was folded in upon herself
black as anthracite

Children, oblivious
had flattened her back

yet she lived
when I toppled the stone
when I pressed my fingers
into her sarcophagus mud
and pried her free;

she shook once
and walked like a drunken man,
her long weaving neck
dizzy with degradation

and her down, now
transformed
white.

How happy did I think
this remembered gift
should feel
as her beak bore down
on shafts of plume

yet nothing like joy
ever swept her wings.

Word Work

This sweltering labour of restraint
as the muscles in my mouth
dam up the ripeness
is more arduous than any job
I have ever done.

Even that scalding July in Ontario
when there were not enough
strawberries in the field
to make a farmer smile
or pay my way to the West coast,
my knees blistered
from crawling in grit.

I have thumbed my way back
into the consummate world
so many times
yet always ignorant
of the circumscription of tidal pools
and the way the ocean squanders
what it cannot use,
of the hourglass
its straight waist
and cinched bulbs,
how every grain
must scrape through.

This work of words
pens us in
        and out
drowns us
in our own flooding eruptions,
seeds our pink tongues
heavily with sand
then demands we know
when and how
to hold them.

Fontainebleau

As we cross the road under the buzz of neon
that strips the sky leaving indelible
gashes, you rush up the court
red wine in a bulb
your face emptying, a tulip kissing
my bleeding mouth
holding my tongue inside
a seed, to find you.

Trucks pass, grass blades cut
the night rolling us into the park,
the swings, the slide
all of a sudden the moon
crashes in the maples;
we ask:
could it be aliens?

but fear the exploding
booby trap blossoms
of love.

Windsor Park

To mark its shrinking
I come back to this park every year
more than thirty summers
after I'd said good-bye
for the last time.

I wanted to forget
how small I felt in the grassy
palms of this city

where boys grow taller than poplars
shoulder to shoulder
and girls collect
china and jewelry
do their nails
some mornings
go to church.

In the centre
I felt the smallest,
snow punishing with whiteness
colours I could no longer see, and
the trees barely started,
through every season
my arms and legs
went missing
even smoke refused to touch.

And somewhere here on my way
to one particular theft
I lost, my magic
blew like newspaper over peaking hills, back
towards the housing projects.

Nowhere on earth was ever
as hollow or held such weight,
or ground me down to flint from such a height.

How did I stand, afterward?
Walk that distance to here?

(While maples and pines have eaten all that,
space and nature always grow back more generous)

Still

I can't forget this small green rapture.

Tecumseh

When we first arrived in Windsor
we didn't know the
name Tecumseh

a street stretching across
the city like a wise snake
burning black as bonfires.

My brother found stone
arrowheads buried
like bullets in rough clay
around our porch;

we didn't know
houses could be built
on angry bones.

Sometimes at night
that year when the entire
neighbourhood slept
I'd look out of my window
in moonlight, see

this copper man.

In our subdivision
people started to divorce, go
crazy, die.
Not one of us knew the first thing about
dreams or visions or where
to begin
stamping them out.

Genesis

In this abyssal zone where hotspurs stew
there is a derelict piscine poet
pariah of piranhas, outcast of sole.

Rows of buttons light his hull
flickering his phosphorescence
for he in an electric daze gestated this world alive

jaded by the hunt he vomited
duplicitous fish into heaven
strung them together with silicon cord

unaware of his gentle art
the magic of a mawkish mind unhinged

himself, a lonely god
to imagine out of loneliness
his likeness in stars

and pitch beneath them, an afterthought
of finless, tailless miscreations
arising at right angles

without gills, flapping
across dust like hammers
bubbles brought beyond

the pale, scattering like minnows
and once begun, twirling off gods like rhymes

pressed life beneath their cyanide feet

claiming the generations as their own.

Bog man

You curl, a log, burnt
black in your Danish
bog, 2000 years have left you
preserved, but faceless
contoured bone
that shows your resolution
on the night you drowned
a gourd pressed to your heart
your thoughts as visible
as your hands, grasping
because you will never taste its sweetness
you cleave
beneath the reeds and rushes
to savour this everlasting
paradox.

Slack Farm

The looters paid ten thousand dollars
drilled promiscuous shovels
through inacquiescent earth

from the sky one could see
a pitted wasteland
craters larger than the tractors

they carried off bones and feathers
left behind broken pottery
shattered jaws
artifacts of people who believed
earth/
    and spirit
could never be divided
    who believed
land/
    and people
could never be sold.

Second Skin

Last night I woke from my coma
after years of avoiding the attack

the cur who split my belly like a sour plum
chopped my face in three

I woke asking
"What year is this?" and all around my mouth, I felt
the stitches.

I couldn't recall his crooked teeth
more intimate than birth twisting in my belly

what made his ravaging closeness run
me through

although his thoughts
did single me out as target.

I woke like one receiving a shock
or a blessing, without him

one who has earned amnesia
and is offered a second skin.

Early Vivisection in an Ontario Heritage Home

I woke again last night
certain I had chopped a man to blocks
in the basement of a house
I owned years ago
in Ontario.

After
burying him with fallen brick
I forgot about it, sold the house
moved out west where I told everyone
I needed a change.

In darkness, this morning,
for at least an hour
I tried piecing it together:

you don't just forget
a thing like that

a body does not
just disappear
into your head

you don't just
hack a life apart
over something you
would rather no one sees.

After tortured re-construction
there was nothing solid to confess

invisible blocks, translucent bricks
I carried their silent weight all day
the heaviness of knowing
there would never be enough passion
to warrant the caress
of such a sharp and savage axe.

Vivisection in a Rwandan Orphanage

they have cut me
with their machetes
sliced my nose, my throat
trenches of scar
sewn over my cheek

extend below my tattered ear

pattern my head
they have cut me
into the blood imbued
pictures I draw
for rich Americans
the pictures I draw
of my family
the pictures I see
when I close my eyes

Indite

Some mornings I lie
as still as a needle
on his prickly blackberry fingers
lick the design of a story
the design of a robber
whose voice is as blue
as his beard.

He will sing into my own gleaming sharpness
his song will be his kiss
his song will be his fascination
dripping sweet blackberry ink
from his lips.

She carries the black birds

in her glass mountain
absent of cornfields
her glass mountain
that is glass or ice or
some transparent substance
filled with birds

they grow spontaneous like flocks
of wild black cancers cursing
the damage she does herself, cursing
the flesh she gives
their food

they scold her, soil her, suck her tits
bitter, ravage her
children grown strong
in one quilled-eclipse
that has erupted her.

Eclipse

In Tahiti they are making love
above the world.

Ebullient voyeur visitors
hug pinhole projectors
close to their rattling chests
they peep in tom-tom drum unction
guard their orbs
against the sun/moon foreplay
and ogle at the passions' journey
over walls of cardboard crate.

Bashful crescents blink
beneath the bushiness of palms,
belts of alabaster
ripple,
blush and stretch
across the buildings
in the cardboard box
a string of beads, an offering
of a diamond ring, sparkles and the
moon's shadow mounts
her consort
photosphere
consummate
with solar shadow.

Turned on onlookers   turn
birds faint from the amethyst sky
hibiscus flowers fold
bees, wild in the climax
of this cool, still butt
land dizzy
and the antediluvian
pulse of silence
thumps with the duration of stone.

Moving back home
the voyeurs think of their safe
civilization
places where they've witnessed pornographic acts
the slippery shafts
of partial light
with cold and well-scoped
lenses.

Collector

Hungry ravens inched over the bones until
they glistened like polished teeth
the rib cage becoming
a prison of oblong insects
we poked without sticks.

Later, you took the carcass
home, a trophy as bright
as any gold angel you hid
in your secret drawer
of stolen pornography.

Your left hand spilled around
the clean contours, hunting
obsolete hollows
ruthless with pleasure
for what
it felt like to possess something
so harmlessly naked.

No. 4

He stood at the apartment window
half naked?
all naked?
hair curling
under fingers, square-
nailed, I imagined
from the bus

night's tar
he'd invited
to unfasten
his curtains
dropping
those fingers
touching, I imagined

past a curve
in the road
a stretch of sand
impossible to blink
or turn away
surprise
in myself and a man
watching
these transit forensics
pulling a cord
getting off.

Fan

The plumed band of androgynous godlings
bolt for the backstage, pierced and peacock-feathered
tattooed above the eyes
racing the retinue of crop-topped, copper-belted
angels
whose jeans (so tight, so white)
make wishbones of their wishing thighs,
the band weary having frequented
numerous psychedelic spheres
cannot recall the nympheans who have
eaten sequins
to taste the iridescent
flesh of stars
still they gather
                and open
follow after in a lunula
of shimmering green eyes
wanting
      more.

(Hockey i)

Sleepy from my dream at eleven
that hangs on my back
still kissing the flesh

my landlady tells me
she will be watching the game.

The game?

> The game!
> Everyone
> in the world
> knows what game
> and it's good to
> see you finally
> alive at eleven.

But I'm not
of the world
my dead lips burble.

Upstairs again, my dream and I
crawl back to the still
warm regions
of bed.

(Hockey ii)

Red maple leaves
painted on large white bed sheets
falling from honking
cars and vans into congestion

while police with spinning cherries
eat pizza
and everyone thinks
at this moment
they are at least in part
Canadian

Greek, Indian, Spanish, Japanese
delis and restaurants
in this four-block span
of Broadway.

Tutored to "O Canada's"
tonelessness
tugged tightly into
self-conscious mouths
that would not make a scene
on their own.

The splitting screams
of students
allow a crack of light and

life from their faces
inside the stores
the cynics scowl
"how American!"

It rolls in the road
like a shower of
cast off loonies, this golden
hysteria.

Spirit that can always find a way
through the blood
to the fingers
from the fingers to the pen
from the pen
to the white, white sheet
a flag to explicate
and surrender
everything
that otherwise
at the end of the day
would just be so much more
fatigue.

Chyna

Her biceps flesh out an Everest
Chyna, pro-announced like vagina
an im-posing Asian country
and a fine bustable crock
"Goddess Mother of the World"
Wrestling Federation's ninth wonder

from scanty hides of doeskin and Alaskan sable
breasts bombastic
moon the coliseum
wayfarer, Chyna
hammer-holds encephalitic dicks

herds pucker in her crush.

"We love yas Chyna!"
die hards boom overhead
a four-year-old in black leather
passes a spitting image of her hero
spiked dominatrix
choker winking from her throat
heavenly bodies cluster
around stunt flying ropes
eyes cleave
to Chyna
con-tender Chyna
first queen bruiser

to burst muscle bound from a pink ghetto
and end up intercontinental champ

she bares the ass she broke for Playboy
a pin-up pinning it all
on the air brushed mat

the hair, the face, the name
the body, a rock pumped gazing stock
with soft porn pyramids
peaking just beyond
the next title
the next count
the next scrap.

Wendy

(i)

Saving lost boys
didn't she grow bitter?
Darning pillow slips by
open windows
on nights so full
of fire denying her
moist lips pleasure.

She always knew
she would never belong
no matter how well
she slayed pirates, yet still
well into old age
her mind could not abandon
its most outrageous lust.

Her clouded eyes observed auras of
frigid moons
while somewhere boys
built forts of steel
smashing iconic
pendulums out of time.

(ii)

Wanting to fly
without strings
her arms extended and rocked
like logan stones as
window ledges pulled her
sideways
bartering her life to earth.

Nightdress swelling passionate
ruffles around her foxy red tail
exposing her sharp
berry bush ridicule.

Afterwards it would take an eternity
for one respectable man
to make her
wife, transform those
broken ledges to barricades
breed her to
the ground.

Anne Morrow Lindbergh

Almost one hundred years old
and your nightgown
is a pink, satin parachute
you arrange,
impatient for flight

ascending the stratosphere
ahead of time

forty-eight hours
to Valentine's day
a nurse's watch stops

Charles
and the baby now grown, wave
from the heart strewn field
your own bright heart
a compass, landing

"my little embroidered, beribboned
world is smashed," you hear
your young voice
love

like wind that rushes
past your white flying cap,
weeps through the inlet

of loaded rose goggles
landscapes of cold blood
paint you
the empyrean navigator
whose hard-
ship
cannot be reconciled
with transatlantic flights

the first American woman
with a license
to glide
who paid a king's ransom
for her dead child

at certain altitudes
collisions are bound to occur
and nothing remains intact.

Charles and the baby waving
beyond
the run way

pink satin clouds soaring and
still

rising from your bed
restless to break.

Eve's Game

This is the secret
we will never know,
the secret bough

the one we played on
whose fruit
at first even He welcomed
because it felt holy
and clean;

there was nothing
but our naked bodies
our animal heads
twisting to the hills
to listen

yet inside
I always felt the islands breaking,
pink lips and tongues spilling
to oceans,
landscapes rolling to words
we couldn't tell Him
because we believed He loved us then
even after
when it was gone

words failed:

some mountains
never can be said

Undertow

Red snakes in the twist
of tree limbs
branches of water
waiting to tickle
the place light has
transformed the ocean white

under stones
two faces are kissing
her head tilts back
his hair is a mane of fire

their love, merging
to orange hysteria
straining to green
passing the sky.

French Beach

Girls leap
like crescents over slick moss,
evoking rock
music soundlessly
in chasms hollowed by waters' tempo
days fall between raucous repose,
as one glistening sea lion
breaks to listen.

Buchanan Tower

Curtains twirl like jigging skirts
out of window hollows

beneath the stairs
bikes pour through air

and spin
like campus swallows

grey-eyed clouds
race open-mouthed

and paint
the pavement's luster

leaf bugs
in the throes of love

lift off
with every bluster.

The Mushroom Picker

It is a straight cut
from here to Vancouver across
the native carpet of forest the
isolate, grey
berries like new-born bullets
on the moss

I carry my scissors in hand
and always leave signs in
places I have trailed

my legs are cocked waiting
to spring on, grace

the hidden fungus
that tunnels
has phallic heads
without religion
like nuns' cornets in autumn

I take them

quiet, fluid, clean of soot.

Lilacs

Today I held you
in my mind
like the first lilacs
I held in my fist.

Soft as small velvet cups
sipped from ether
they hung over the pointed pillars
of a white picket fence.

Before I took them, I stood beside the bush
drinking in their purple essence
knowing I would always
love lilacs.

This is your map of the world

contoured with mountain
ranges, where you remember being small
and your body's beginning
under the slack tar
of a Sunday sea

green vine stars twine
in the wet laurel, crawl across
the giant's grave.

You invented then buried him under this humus
with dead birds and hamsters, tulip and iris bulbs

from concrete to concrete
his fragrances rise
in rain

your cartographic pencil
skids across a dearth of oceans,
an asphalt meadow
a jungle gym.

You take x-rays of this place you tore from
crevice-filled with emerald recollections;
the corners containing all
you carry
treasures that torture,
blueprints of you

walking away.

Clytie

(1)

Under this wide, whole moon
only the fir is witnessing
this earth it runs its fingers through

and the sky I climb
collecting seeds
of your voice.

If I could speak
I would tell you
bodies are just as holy

as any prayer,
invite you
to bathe

in this light river
of soft needles
and leaves.

Flesh is the fire
of god's path
not the pulpit

where they'd damn me
for preaching
the nature of love.

(II)

All night I turn
holding you in my hand

a pink quartz heart
and a coin you gave me once;

I tuck them both into my pillow slip
where morning won't illuminate

the reason
I still can't let you go.

Gum stuck to the pavement
by the weight of passing traffic,

everywhere there are people
I imagine you loving

with that love
you emit like oxygen,

the memory gnawing at my lungs
jealous of everything that breathes

and everything that doesn't
but finds its way to you

like a glinting garbage pail
and the bright books on your shelf

I would trade places just
to feel your finger on my spine

Gladly, I would stop breathing
if it meant I might be held by you.

(III)

It has been such a long time
since you have written

and the days are shortening
and the skies are filling up with grey

and I wonder if it's something
that I did or didn't do, that has caused you

to abandon
the summer

to invite red leaves
and black feathers to fall

instead of me
over your path.

(IV)

If I could speak
I might ask you

if you'd ever thought
of kissing me

over the black moss
of stone;

my torture has become
not knowing

if this love exists
in me alone;

like sand, the past
loses its impression

and as I see you less
there are more questions....

(v)

The calyx of my grief
is like one large brown eye
set off by yellow lashes
watching you in the groove of your day
cross the sky

seeing the "I" in everything I've written,
there are few places that become as selfish as love
or as distressing as its constant cry to be kissed and
     carried,
roots and stalk twisting always towards you.

I must grow beyond the moan of myself,
forsake the fragrance of your warmth
and send instead the light of my own perfume
out towards you

to hold you always
in the brightness of my thoughts
without needing you to see me
or trying to convince you
why it is you should.

(VI)

There is no place left to go
the flesh has ruptured
the toughest seed casing

enticing the world's wound
to fall into this gash

heavy with hunger
hatching sufferings multiple
as aphids

always carrying
love's mute burden
in the bowl of a flower.

Night Before New Year's

And I waste my time
looking you up
on the net
nothing better to do
but consult a battery
of spirits about our future
if I will exist
into morning
or melt
like ice chips
on god's lips
nothing better to do
but imagine you
re-create you.

Angel Consciousness

If it weren't for dreams
that held me to this course

I would leave this place
and pour my spirit out

into other lives
celestial amnesia

would imbue
with emptiness

for the load of love
carried by an angel

is as heavy
as the habiliments of hell.

Angel I

Today, in the Safeway
I recognized Uriel
standing before me in the line

his red basket
swinging on his dark wing
like a berry

his black cloak's hem
collecting all
the earthly crumbs.

Pushing two kiwi fruit
over that moving highway
his bone-white face stretched

to accommodate the cashier.
Where is it
that angels keep their pockets

and why do their hands
pant and fumble
searching for precise change?

He might take me with him
on the horse he has tied on 10th
if only I were not so critical
of animals
and their habits.

Angel II

Again, in the pub
Uriel is sitting
slumped over beer

wings like black bed linen
falling over the bar
chin so low

I can not see
his lovely
eyes

pining for
that well-dressed
pleather-panted flirt.

How I wish
I were young and pretty
to drink with Uriel

feel the softness of his feathers
touch my face

make him happy.

I want to tell him
she never loved you,
she even used to call you names

knowing it will make no difference
knowing one can not warn an angel.

Angel III

Dear Ann Landers,
I am in trouble.

I have fallen in love
with the angel of death.

How do I get him
to notice me

to want to drive me home
or even take me back to his place?

I will go anywhere he says;

it's bad Ann
there is a whole planet of women
dragging on his chain

and a wife
dear lord

who doesn't want to share him.

I know I should just wake up
and smell the coffee

but the pain, Ann,
the pain of wanting

just to lie beneath his wings.

The Awakening of a Love Struck Flea

I am a speck, a fleck, a flea
coming to terms with this dog's body
I have suddenly found myself riding upon

a spot, smaller than a pin head
a fraction to the left
of a loose whisker

this is my space in the world
and the only place
I have ever really wanted

because all I ever wanted
was to be close to your flesh
close though I never thought

about my loneliness
loping along and, being in the pleasure
of your body's heat;

I never knew until yesterday
exactly where I stood

still I can not disembark
because now I have fallen in love
with blood

yours and mine
it makes no difference to the tongue
that speaks it

is it any wonder I wait
for the sure suicide
of a sneeze?

to be spewed and shaken clean
cast into the black of the glistening road
slick with rain.

Because you know where these thoughts are coming from

(some people spend
their lives believing
they are guilty
of a dirty mind)

I need you to tell me
why a thought can
strangle a heart,

make a wide vine of
morning glory creep
over a forest of oak.

I need you to tell me
why each morning begins with you
and each day fills
like a cup
overflowing
with thoughts of you

why these tides
cannot be quelled or burned
in the flames of my white
candles

or sent to heaven
in a fist of prayer;

it is my dirty
exhalations
I cannot prevent,

my body's curse of feeling
the other half
of what I've been blessed with,

the breath
to blow myself
apart.

Suicide #1

After you left
I bought a knife
and carved your initials
into the bark
of my wrist

knowing no bird would ever visit
or lay her eggs
in the palms of my hands

knowing the weight
of small sad treasures
and how their absences
leave their marks.

Suicide #2

All winter my wish
is for the cedar cords to topple
from the trucks on 10th
and strike an end
to all this
unanesthetized amputation;
lungs clouded by the blackness
of your leaving, again
car lights speeding
without stopping
the you upon my lips
rain that smells and tastes like
the inky berry blood
of Belladonna
growing in the forest
you've abandoned.

Suicide #3

This is the way you die
of a broken heart
one night at two
you hear the man you can't stop thinking of
shut the door
you remember the last time
he saw you and how
for a moment he couldn't find
your name
like his keys or his wallet
in a sleazy motel
shoved down the crack
of a love seat
while the rain outside
stabbed the earth
and you sat there
waiting
for him to
fish
you
up.

Extract

When the hot iron
pressed its print
into my cotton shirt
there was nothing
to remove its dark tattoo
but scissors

now I turn thoughts over
like kitchen drawers
searching for the right utensil
to cut you from my sleeve

this is how I've learned
to fashion scars—

when I make you leave
I will always see
you're missing.

Easter

Someone died
a car accident's the usual way
although the newspapers found
a man who had been asphyxiated
underground.

We tried not to think
of the place; we cut him away
as surgeons
took his organs

(yet still we could not stop
ourselves from thinking)

I did not see the table
where he entered your body
but upstairs while you slept
other men looked like you.

Fine brown hair, defiant eye
sharing more than phenotype

    now
     he lived;

the day was grey and pink
the sky made of plasticine

the sun blinding less
than hail both falling in my
eyes together as I walked.

People and dogs abandoning the trail
while I continued.

Then afterwards together
on your hospital bed
without questions

both of us bold and joyous
drinking the precious pleasure of
orange life, as if
the entire earth had crumbled
in upon us, yet still
in our reckless wonder
we were

breathing.

Décor

I took you
to the horror shop
where the man
locks the doors
from the inside,

showed you glass cases filled
with death:

(small horror huts we could collect. My favourite
of mud and long grass, skulls silver thimbles
dancing its perimeter, windows of solid black,
open-mouthed doors where we crawled laughing
our bellies blue   brushing shoulders,
rolling on bottles, on   bodies, under swinging
canopies of snapping ghosts' girdles).

When laughter died

I asked: "Does this mean anything to you?"
Your eyes, great obsidian mirrors, had stopped
no passion nor sweetness
reflected.

Death wants to die

to fold expired, framed

over fields of glinting green
where horses ate sweet
from our palms
and the mother pink sky hurt
us to remember

yet now he wants to die
send healing hopes
to hell, roll randy earth
face down, riding
his rampage to rigor mortis.

You are the empty book

heavily, silently
you open, people
imagine you
in days.

In decades all
your pages ache
and come apart
what is left at last
when the light poem
hot and round
dressed in sound
carrying her skirts
in and out
flies free is the song that breaks glass
cases that move in clouds
she is the music
of every secret wish,
down in valleys and
black ravines; is the
fire that bakes into
being, new plants
rising grateful, rings
in the mossy trees,

the black pupil,
the push and pull
and when you break out joyous
from your pages

you are full.

Acknowledgements

I wish to acknowledge the poets at the University of British Columbia who encouraged, inspired, and sustained me: George McWhirter, Carl Leggo, and Renee Norman. I also wish to thank the University of British Columbia's Creative Writing program's graduate poetry class of 2000-2001 for critiques both useful and kind. Special thanks go to Eric Henderson who has been my first reader over these many long years.

Some of the poems in this volume previously appeared in the following journals:

"Fade" and "Vivisection in a Rwandan Orphanage" in *Canadian Woman Studies/les cahiers de la femme*; "Clean" in *echolocation*; "Anne Morrow Lindbergh" and "Wendy" in *Room of One's Own*; "Ties" in *Grain*; "She Scrubs Her Hands" in *Contemporary Verse 2*; and "Tecumseh" in *Event*.

Photo: Claudia Molina

Madeline Sonik is a writer and anthologist whose fiction, poetry, and creative non-fiction have appeared in literary journals internationally. Her first novel, *Arms,* and her collection of short fiction, *Drying the Bones,* were published by Nightwood Editions. A children's novel, *Belinda and the Dustbunnys,* was published by Hodgepog Books. Her anthologies include *When I Was a Child* and *Entering the Landscape* (Oberon Press), and *Fresh Blood:New Canadian Gothic Fiction* (Turnstone Press). She holds a Ph.D. in Education, an MFA in Creative Writing and an MA in Journalism.